John Facey

Jumping Into PHP

Jumping Into PHP

Jumping Into PHP

A quick start to learning PHP

By John Facey

Introduction to PHP
10

Variables and Data Types
15

Control Structures
25

Introduction Error handling
70

Database connectivity
76

Creating and executing queries in PHP
78

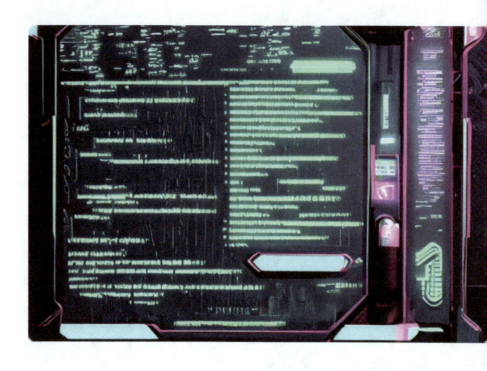

Introduction to PHP

PHP is a popular server-side scripting language used for web development. It is an acronym for "PHP: Hypertext Preprocessor". PHP is open source software and is free to download and use.

What is PHP?

PHP is a powerful programming language that allows developers to create dynamic and interactive websites. PHP can be embedded into HTML code or be used to generate HTML code. PHP is a server-side language, which means that it is executed on the server and the results are sent to the client's browser. PHP is a flexible language that can be used for a wide range of web development requirements.

Why PHP?

PHP is one of the most widely used programming languages for web development. Here are some reasons why:

- PHP is free and open source.

- PHP is easy to learn and use.

- PHP is supported by a large community of developers.

- PHP is cross-platform, which means that it can run on different operating systems.

- PHP is compatible with many databases, including MySQL, PostgreSQL, and Oracle.

- PHP offers a vast range of libraries and frameworks that can be used to build complex web applications with ease.

Getting Started with PHP

To start using PHP, you will need a web server that supports PHP. You can download PHP from the official PHP website, and you can find web servers that support PHP from web hosting providers. There are several web servers that support PHP, including Apache, Nginx, and Microsoft IIS.

Once you have PHP and a web server set up, you can start writing PHP code. PHP code is typically embedded into HTML code using special tags. For example, to display the current date using PHP, you can use the following code:

```php
<p>Today's date is <?php echo date('Y-m-d'); ?></p>
```

This code will display the current date in the format "YYYY-MM-DD". PHP code can also be used to interact with databases, create user authentication systems, and handle file uploads and downloads.

PHP is a powerful and versatile programming language that is widely used for web development. It is free, easy to learn, and supported by a large community of developers. If you are interested in web development, learning PHP is a great place to start. With its vast range of libraries and frameworks, PHP can be used to build simple websites or complex web applications with ease.

Variables and Data Types

Variables are used to store data in PHP. A variable can hold different types of data, such as numbers, strings, or arrays. In PHP, variables are denoted with a dollar sign ($) followed by the variable name.

Declaring Variables

To declare a variable in PHP, you simply need to assign a value to it using the assignment operator (=). For example:

```php
$name = "John";
$age = 25;
```

In this example, `$name` is a variable that holds a string value of "John", and `$age` is a variable that holds a numeric value of 25.

Data Types

PHP supports several data types, including:

Strings

Strings are used to represent text in PHP. A string is a sequence of characters enclosed in quotes. Strings can be declared using single quotes ('') or double quotes (""). For example:

In this example, `$name` is a string variable that holds the value "John", and `$message` is a string variable that holds the value "Hello, John!".

```
$name = 'John';
$message = "Hello, $name!";
```

Integers

Integers are used to represent whole numbers in PHP. For example:

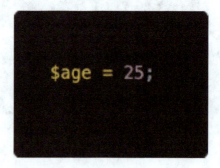

In this example, `$age` is an integer variable that holds the value 25.

Floats

Floats are used to represent numbers with decimal points in PHP. For example:

```php
$price = 9.99;
```

, `$price` is a float variable that holds the value 9.99.

Booleans

Booleans are used to represent true or false values in PHP. For example:

```php
$is_valid = true;
```

In this example, `$is_valid` is a boolean variable that holds the value true.

Arrays

Arrays are used to store multiple values in PHP. An array can hold values of different data types, such as strings, integers, or floats. For example:

```php
$fruits = array('apple', 'banana', 'orange');
```

In this example, $fruits is an array variable that holds three string values: "apple", "banana", and "orange".

Variable Scope

Variable scope refers to the visibility of a variable within a PHP script. There are two types of variable scope in PHP: global and local.

Global Variables

Global variables are declared outside of a function and can be accessed from anywhere in the script. For example:

```php
$name = "John";

function say_hello() {
    global $name;
    echo "Hello, $name!";
}

say_hello();
```

In this example, $name is a global variable that is accessible from within the say_hello() function using the global keyword.

Local Variables

Local variables are declared inside of a function and can only be accessed from within that function. For example:

```php
function say_hello() {
    $name = "John";
    echo "Hello, $name!";
}

say_hello();
```

In this example, `$name` is a local variable that is only accessible from within the `say_hello()` function.

Variables and data types are fundamental concepts in PHP. Variables are used to store data, and data types determine the type of data that can be stored in a variable. Understanding variable scope is also important for writing clean and organized PHP code. By mastering variables and data types, you'll be well on your way to becoming a proficient PHP developer.

Control Structures

Control structures are used to control the flow of execution in a PHP script. They allow you to make decisions, repeat actions, and perform different actions based on different conditions.

Conditional Statements

Conditional statements allow you to make decisions in your PHP code based on whether a certain condition is true or false. The most common conditional statements in PHP are `if`, `else`, and `elseif`.

if Statement

The `if` statement is used to perform an action if a certain condition is true. For example:

```php
$age = 25;

if ($age > 18) {
    echo "You are an adult.";
}
```

In this example, the `if` statement checks if `$age` is greater than 18. If it is, then the script will output "You are an adult."

else Statement

The `else` statement is used to perform an action if the `if` statement is false. For example:

```php
$age = 15;

if ($age > 18) {
    echo "You are an adult.";
} else {
    echo "You are not an adult.";
}
```

In this example, if the `$age` variable is less than or equal to 18, then the script will output "You are not an adult."

elseif Statement

The `elseif` statement is used to perform a different action based on a different condition if the `if` statement is false. For example:

```php
$age = 15;

if ($age > 18) {
    echo "You are an adult.";
} elseif ($age < 18) {
    echo "You are a minor.";
} else {
    echo "You are exactly 18.";
}
```

In this example, if the `$age` variable is less than 18, then the script will output "You are a minor." If `$age` is exactly 18, then the script will output "You are exactly 18."

Looping Structures

Looping structures allow you to repeat a certain action multiple times based on a certain condition. The most common looping structures in PHP are `for`, `while`, and `do-while`.

for Loop

The `for` loop is used to repeat a certain action a certain number of times. For example:

```php
for ($i = 0; $i < 10; $i++) {
    echo $i;
}
```

In this example, the `for` loop will repeat the `echo $i;` statement 10 times, with `$i` starting at 0 and incrementing by 1 each time.

while Loop

The `while` loop is used to repeat a certain action while a certain condition is true. For example:

```
$i = 0;

while ($i < 10) {
    echo $i;
    $i++;
}
```

In this example, the `while` loop will repeat the `echo $i;` statement as long as `$i` is less than 10, with `$i` starting at 0 and incrementing by 1 each time.

do-while Loop

The `do-while` loop is similar to the `while` loop, but it will always execute the loop at least once, even if the condition is false. For example:

```
$i = 0;

do {
    echo $i;
    $i++;
} while ($i < 10);
```

In this example, the `do-while` loop will repeat the `echo $i;` statement as long as `$i` is less than 10, with `$i` starting at 0 and incrementing by 1 each time. However, even if `$i` is initially greater than or equal to 10, the `echo $i;` statement will still be executed once.

Control structures are essential for controlling the flow of execution in your PHP scripts. Conditional statements allow you to make decisions based on certain conditions, while looping structures allow you to repeat actions based on certain conditions. By mastering control structures, you'll be able to write more complex and powerful PHP scripts.

What is a function in PHP?

A function in PHP is a block of code that can be executed repeatedly. Functions are used to encapsulate reusable code, and they can make your code more modular and efficient.

How to define a function in PHP?

To define a function in PHP, you use the `function` keyword. The syntax for defining a function is as follows:

```
function function_name(parameters) {
    // Code to be executed
}
```

- `function_name`: The name of the
  function.

- `parameters`: The list of parameters
  that the function accepts.

- `Code to be executed`: The code that
  will be executed when the function is
  called.

How to call a function in PHP?

To call a function in PHP, you use the
function name followed by parentheses.
The parentheses can contain the
arguments that the function expects.

```
function_name(arguments);
```

For example, the following code defines a function called `greet()` that takes a name as an argument:

```php
function greet($name) {
    echo "Hello, $name!";
}
```

The following code calls the `greet()` function:

```php
greet("John Doe");
```

This code will output the following text: Hello, John Doe!

Parameters in PHP functions

Functions can take parameters, which are values that are passed to the function when it is called. Parameters can be used to customize the behavior of the function.

The syntax for declaring a parameter is as follows:

```
parameter_name : data_type
```

- `parameter_name`: The name of the parameter.

- `data_type`: The data type of the parameter.

```
function sum($x, $y) {
    return $x + $y;
}
```

The following code calls the `sum()` function:

```
$result = sum(10, 20);
```

This code will assign the value 30 to the variable `$result`.

Return values in PHP functions

Functions can return values. The return value is the value that is returned by the function when it is finished executing.

The syntax for returning a value from a function is as follows:

```
return value;
```

- `value`: The value to be returned.

For example, the following code defines a function called `get_name()` that returns the name of the current user:

```
function get_name() {
    return $_SESSION['username'];
}
```

The following code calls the `get_name()` function:

```
$name = get_name();
```

This code will assign the value of the `username` session variable to the variable `$name`.

Built-in functions in PHP

PHP comes with a large number of built-in functions. These functions can be used to perform a variety of tasks, such as string manipulation, mathematical operations, & file I/O.

To find out more about the built-in functions in PHP, you can refer to the PHP manual: https://www.php.net/manual/en/.

Functions are an essential part of any PHP program. They can be used to encapsulate reusable code, make your code more modular and efficient, and improve readability.

Arrays

An array in PHP is a data structure that stores multiple values in a single variable. Arrays are used to store related data, such as the names and ages of students, the prices of products, or the scores of a game.

Types of arrays in PHP

There are two types of arrays in PHP:

- **Numeric arrays:** Numeric arrays are indexed by integers. The first element in the array has an index of 0, the second element has an index of 1, and so on.

- **Associative arrays:** Associative arrays are indexed by strings. The index can be any string, such as a name, a product code, or a date.

Creating arrays in PHP

There are two ways to create arrays in PHP:

```
$array = array(1, 2, 3);
```

- Using the `array()` function:

The `array()` function can also be used to create associative arrays. To do this, you pass a list of key-value pairs to the function. The keys must be strings, and the values can be of any type.

Using square brackets:

```
$array = [1, 2, 3];
```

The `array()` function can also be used to create associative arrays. To do this, you pass a list of key-value pairs to the function. The keys must be strings, and the values can be of any type.

```php
$array = array('name' => 'John Doe', 'age' => 30);
```

Accessing array elements in PHP

You can access the elements of an array using their index or key.

To access an element of a numeric array, you use the index enclosed in square brackets. For example, the following code will print the value of the first element in the array:

```php
echo $array[0];
```

To access an element of an associative array, you use the key enclosed in curly braces. For example, the following code will print the value of the name key in the array:

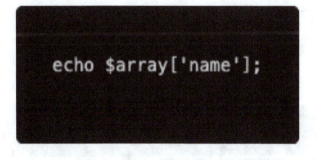

```
echo $array['name'];
```

Adding and removing elements from arrays in PHP

You can add elements to an array using the `array_push()` function. The `array_push()` function takes an array and a list of elements as its arguments. The elements are added to the end of the array.

```
array_push($array, 4, 5, 6);
```

You can remove elements from an array using the `array_pop()` function. The `array_pop()` function removes the last element from the array.

```
$value = array_pop($array);
```

You can also remove elements from an array by their index or key. To do this, you use the `unset()` function. The `unset()` function takes the index or key of the element to be removed as its argument.

```
unset($array[0]);
unset($array['name']);
```

Sorting arrays in PHP

You can sort the elements of an array in ascending or descending order using the `sort()` function. The `sort()` function takes an array as its argument.

```
sort($array);
```

To sort the elements of an array in descending order, you can use the `rsort()` function.

```
rsort($array);
```

Iterating through arrays in PHP

You can iterate through the elements of an array using a for loop or a foreach loop.

To iterate through the elements of an array using a for loop, you can use the following syntax:

```php
for ($i = 0; $i < count($array); $i++) {
    echo $array[$i];
}
```

To iterate through the elements of an array using a foreach loop, you can use the following syntax:

```php
foreach ($array as $value) {
    echo $value;
}
```

Arrays are a powerful data structure that can be used to store and manipulate data in PHP. They are an essential part of any PHP program.

Object-oriented programming

Object-oriented programming (OOP) is a programming paradigm that treats data and the functions that operate on that data as objects. In OOP, objects are created to represent things in the real world, such as cars, people, or animals.

Classes and objects

In PHP, a class is a blueprint for creating objects. A class defines the properties and methods of an object. A property is a data attribute of an object, and a method is a function that is associated with an object.

To create a class in PHP, you use the `class` keyword. The syntax for creating a class is as follows:

```
class Classname {
    // Properties
    // Methods
}
```

- Classname: The name of the class.

- Properties: The list of properties of the class.

- Methods: The list of methods of the class.

Creating objects

To create an object from a class, you use the `new` keyword. The syntax for creating an object is as follows:

```
$object = new Classname();
```

- `$object`: The name of the object variable.

- `Classname`: The name of the class.

Accessing object properties and methods

You can access the properties and methods of an object using the dot notation. The syntax for accessing a property is as follows:

```
$object->property_name;
```

The syntax for accessing a method is as follows:

```
$object->method_name();
```

Inheritance

Inheritance is a feature of OOP that allows one class to inherit the properties and methods of another class. The class that inherits the properties and methods is called the **derived class**, and the class that is being inherited from is called the **base class**.

To inherit from a class, you use the `extends` keyword. The syntax for inheriting from a class is as follows:

```
class DerivedClass extends BaseClass {
    // Properties
    // Methods
}
```

Encapsulation

Encapsulation is a feature of OOP that hides the implementation details of an object from the outside world. This makes the object more secure and easier to maintain.

Encapsulation is achieved by using private and protected properties and methods. Private properties and methods can only be accessed from within the class, while protected properties and methods can be accessed from within the class and its subclasses.

Abstraction

Abstraction is a feature of OOP that allows you to create classes that represent the essential features of an object without having to worry about the details of its implementation. This makes it easier to create reusable and maintainable code.

An abstract class is a class that cannot be instantiated. It is used to define the common properties and methods of a set of classes.

Polymorphism

Polymorphism is a feature of OOP that allows you to have different implementations of the same method for different objects. This makes it possible to write code that is more flexible and adaptable to change.

Polymorphism is achieved by using abstract classes and interfaces. An interface is a set of methods that a class must implement.

Introduction File handling

File handling is the process of reading, writing, and managing files on a computer system. PHP provides a number of functions for file handling, including functions for opening, closing, reading, writing, and deleting files.

Opening files in PHP

To open a file in PHP, you use the `fopen()` function. The syntax for opening a file is as follows:

```
$handle = fopen($filename, $mode);
```

- `$filename`: The name of the file to be opened.

- `$mode`: The mode in which the file is to be opened. The mode can be one of the following:

  - `r`: Open the file for reading only.

  - `w`: Open the file for writing only. If the file does not exist, it will be created. If the file does exist, its contents will be erased.

  - `a`: Open the file for appending. The file pointer will be positioned at the end of the file.

- r+: Open the file for reading and writing.

- w+: Open the file for reading and writing. If the file does not exist, it will be created. If the file does exist, its contents will be erased.

- a+: Open the file for reading and appending. The file pointer will be positioned at the end of the file.

Reading files in PHP

To read a file in PHP, you use the `fread()` function. The syntax for reading a file is as follows:

```
$contents = fread($handle, $length);
```

- `$handle`: The file handle returned by the `fopen()` function.

- `$length`: The number of bytes to be read.

The `fread()` function will return the contents of the file as a string. If the end of the file is reached before `$length` bytes have been read, the function will return fewer than $length bytes.

Writing files in PHP

To write to a file in PHP, you use the `fwrite()` function. The syntax for writing to a file is as follows:

```php
$bytes_written = fwrite($handle, $data);
```

- `$handle`: The file handle returned by the `fopen()` function.

- `$data`: The data to be written to the file.

The `fwrite()` function will return the number of bytes that were successfully written to the file.

Closing files in PHP

To close a file in PHP, you use the `fclose()` function. The syntax for closing a file is as follows:

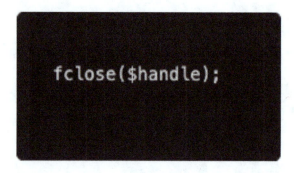

```
fclose($handle);
```

- `$handle`: The file handle returned by the `fopen()` function.

The `fclose()` function will close the file and free up any resources associated with the file.

Other file handling functions in PHP

PHP provides a number of other file handling functions, such as functions for creating, deleting, and renaming files. For more information, you can refer to the PHP manual: https://www.php.net/manual/en/ref.filesystem.php

File handling is a fundamental skill for any PHP developer. By understanding the file handling functions in PHP, you can create applications that can read, write, and manage files on a computer system.

Introduction Error handling

Error handling is the process of detecting and responding to errors in a program. PHP provides a number of features for error handling, including error reporting, error logging, and custom error handlers.

Error reporting in PHP

PHP has a built-in error reporting system that can be used to control the level of detail of the error messages that are displayed. The error reporting level can be set using the `error_reporting()` function. The syntax for setting the error reporting level is as follows:

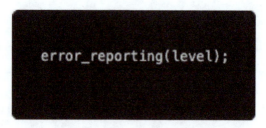

```
error_reporting(level);
```

- `$level`: The error reporting level. The level can be a combination of the following constants:

  - E_ERROR: Fatal errors.

  - E_WARNING: Warnings.

  - E_PARSE: Parse errors.

  - E_NOTICE: Notices.

  - E_ALL: All errors and warnings.

The default error reporting level is E_ALL & ~E_NOTICE. This means that all errors and warnings are reported, except for notices.

Error logging in PHP

PHP also has a built-in error logging system that can be used to log errors to a file. The error log file can be used to troubleshoot errors that occur in a program.

To enable error logging, you can use the error_log() function. The syntax for enabling error logging is as follows:

```
error_log($message, $level, $destination);
```

- `$message`: The error message to be logged.

- `$level`: The error level. The level can be one of the constants listed above.

- `$destination`: The destination of the error log. The destination can be a file name, a URL, or a special value that indicates that the error should be logged to the system error log.

Custom error handlers in PHP

A custom error handler is a function that is called when an error occurs. Custom error handlers can be used to handle errors in a more sophisticated way than the built-in error handling system.

To define a custom error handler, you can use the `set_error_handler()` function. The syntax for defining a custom error handler is as follows:

```
set_error_handler($handler);
```

$handler: The custom error handler function. The function must take three arguments: the error level, the error message, and the error file and line number.

The following is an example of a custom error handler function:

```php
function custom_error_handler($error_level, $error_message, $error_file, $error_line) {
    // Send an email to the developer with the error message.
}
```

Error handling is an important part of any programming language. By understanding the error handling features in PHP, you can create programs that are more reliable and easier to debug.

Database connectivity

Database connectivity is the ability to connect to a database and interact with it. PHP provides a number of functions for database connectivity, including functions for connecting to a database, creating and executing queries, and retrieving data from the database.

Connecting to a database in PHP

To connect to a database in PHP, you use the `mysqli_connect()` function. The syntax for connecting to a database is as follows:

```php
$conn = mysqli_connect($host, $username, $password, $database);
```

- `$host`: The hostname of the database server.

- `$username`: The username for the database.

- `$password`: The password for the database.

- `$database`: The name of the database.

The `mysqli_connect()` function will return a connection handle if the connection is successful. If the connection is not successful, the function will return false.

Creating and executing queries in PHP

Once you have connected to a database, you can create and execute queries using the `mysqli_query()` function. The syntax for creating and executing a query is as follows:

```
$result = mysqli_query($conn, $query);
```

- $conn: The connection handle returned by the `mysqli_connect()` function.

- $query: The SQL query to be executed.

The `mysqli_query()` function will return a result set if the query is successful. If the query is not successful, the function will return false.

Retrieving data from the database in PHP

Once you have executed a query, you can retrieve the data from the result set using the `mysqli_fetch_assoc()` function. The syntax for retrieving data from a result set is as follows:

```
$row = mysqli_fetch_assoc($result);
```

- `$result`: The result set returned by the `mysqli_query()` function.

The `mysqli_fetch_assoc()` function will return an associative array with the data from the current row in the result set. If there are no more rows in the result set, the function will return false.

Closing a database connection in PHP

Once you are finished with a database connection, you should close it using the `mysqli_close()` function. The syntax for closing a database connection is as follows:

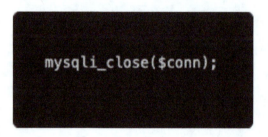

```
mysqli_close($conn);
```

- `$conn`: The connection handle returned by the `mysqli_connect()` function.

Other database connectivity functions in PHP

PHP provides a number of other database connectivity functions, such as functions for fetching data from a result set in a different format, and functions for handling errors that occur during database operations. For more information, you can refer to the PHP manual: https://www.php.net/manual/en/ref.mysqli.php

Database connectivity is an essential skill for any PHP developer. By understanding the database connectivity functions in PHP, you can create applications that can interact with databases.

Operators and Expressions

Operators and expressions are fundamental concepts in PHP. Operators are symbols that represent an action, such as addition or comparison, and expressions are combinations of variables, constants, and operators that evaluate to a value.

Arithmetic Operators

Arithmetic operators are used to perform mathematical calculations in PHP. The basic arithmetic operators are:

- + Addition

- `` Subtraction

- `` Multiplication

- / Division

- % Modulus (remainder of division)

For example:

```php
$x = 10;
$y = 5;

$sum = $x + $y;
$difference = $x - $y;
$product = $x * $y;
$quotient = $x / $y;
$remainder = $x % $y;

echo "Sum: $sum
";
echo "Difference: $difference
";
echo "Product: $product
";
echo "Quotient: $quotient
";
echo "Remainder: $remainder
";
```

This code will output:

```
Sum: 15
Difference: 5
Product: 50
Quotient: 2
Remainder: 0
```

Comparison Operators

Comparison operators are used to compare values in PHP. The comparison operators are:

- == Equal to

- != Not equal to

- < Less than

- > Greater than

- <= Less than or equal to

- >= Greater than or equal to

For example:

```
$x = 10;
$y = 5;

if ($x > $y) {
    echo "$x is greater than $y";
} else {
    echo "$y is greater than or equal to $x";
}
```

This code will output:

```
10 is greater than 5
```

Logical Operators

Logical operators are used to combine multiple conditions in PHP. The logical operators are:

- **&&** And

- **||** Or

- **!** Not

For example:

```php
$x = 10;
$y = 5;

if ($x > $y && $x < 20) {
    echo "$x is greater than $y and less than 20";
} else {
    echo "$x is not greater than $y and less than 20";
}
```

This code will output:

```
10 is greater than 5 and less than 20
```

Assignment Operators

Assignment operators are used to assign values to variables in PHP. The assignment operators are:

- = Assign

- += Add and assign

- = Subtract and assign

- = Multiply and assign

- /= Divide and assign

- %= Modulus and assign

For example:

```php
$x = 10;
$y = 5;

$x += $y;

echo "x is now $x"; // Output: x is now 15
```

Operators and expressions are essential components of PHP. Arithmetic operators are used to perform mathematical calculations, comparison operators are used to compare values, logical operators are used to combine conditions, and assignment operators are used to assign values to variables. By mastering these concepts, you'll be well on your way to becoming a proficient PHP developer.

About the Author

John Facey II - I am a software solutions
architect currently living in Dallas, Texas. I
am well versed in JavaScript, PHP, Node.js,
Salesforce Commerce Cloud and various
other languages and platforms.

John Facey

https://johnfacey.dev

https://github.com/johnfacey